Victorian and Edwa

In the late 19th and early 20th centuries, Sheffield was the most important manufacturing and commercial centre (Leeds being larger), renowned, in particular, for its steel products. As such, it was an important business and tourist destination. Detailed guide books, such as Black's Guide to Yorkshire, were available to help visitors make the most of their stay. Black's was updated each year and included historical facts about local towns and villages, where to stay, what to see and excursions to places of interest.

This booklet combines text relating to Sheffield from Black's Guide, published in 1888, with photographs from postcards and 'magic lantern' projection slides owned by the Keasbury-Gordon Photograph Archive.

It is in three parts. The first is twenty six photographs probably taken between 1890 and 1920; the second, a detailed visitor's guide to Sheffield and the surrounding area, including Wentworth House (Wentworth Woodhouse) and the third, a history and general description of Yorkshire. The text for parts two and three is reproduced from the 1888 guide-book.

The Black's Guide text and the photographs complement each other and enable us to travel back in time to visit this important British city at the height of its manufacturing power. I hope you enjoy the journey.

Andrew Gill

Castle Street

Sheffield Fire Station

Great Central Railway Station

High Street

Midland Railway Station

Moor Head

South Street

Woodseats Tram Terminus

Pye Bank, Woodside

An Industrial Panorama

Fargate

The Town Hall

Dore and Totley Station

Crookes Tram Terminus

Hillsborough Tram Terminus

Nether Green Tram Terminus

Ranmoor

Walkley Tram Terminus

Woodhouse

Coldstream Place, Woodseats

A rainy day in Sheffield in the 1920s

Rockingham Arms, Wentworth

Wentworth House / Wentworth Woodhouse

Wentworth Woodhouse Fire Engine

Wentworth Village

Wentworth Village

A Sheffield Munitions Factory during the First World War

An illustration of Sherwood Forest

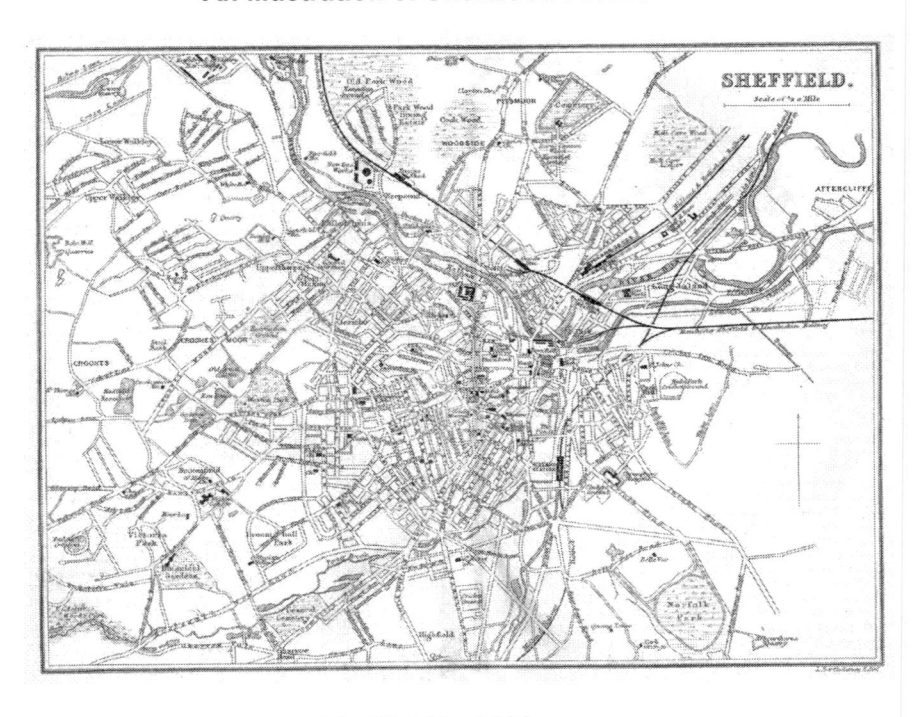

Sheffield in 1888

CITY ARMS OF SHEFFIELD.

SHEFFIELD.

HOTELS.—*The Victoria* (close to the M. S. & L. Station), *Wharncliffe, Imperial, The Maunche, Black Swan, King's Head, Royal*, etc.

Distances.

From York, 46 miles ; Leeds, 39 ; Huddersfield, 26 ; Doncaster, 27¼ ; London, 162½.

Sheffield, "the metropolis of steel," is situated near the confluence of the Don and the Sheaf, at the eastern foot of that extensive range of hills which traverses the centre of the island from Staffordshire to Westmoreland. It is the chief town of the ancient Saxon District of Hallamshire ; and the name is evidently derived from the Sheaf, which here mingles its waters with the Don. Under William the Conqueror, the manor of Sheffield was held by Roger de Busli ; and in the reign of Henry I. it came, with other estates, to the family of De Lavetot. A castle, no vestiges of which remain, was built at a very early period, probably by a member of this family. The castle and manor passed by marriage to the Furnivals, and ultimately to the Talbots, Earls of Shrewsbury. On the failure of heirs-male to that line, it passed by marriage to Thomas Howard, Earl of Arundell and Surrey, with whose heirs it still continues. In 1530, Cardinal Wolsey, having been arrested at Cawood by order of Henry VIII., was brought to the manor-house,* where he remained sixteen days. Here also in 1570 Mary Queen of Scots lay immured for fourteen years—having been delivered over by Elizabeth to the keeping of the Earl of Shrewsbury. In the civil wars, Sheffield declared for the Parliament ; but subsequently surrendered to the Earl of

* Restored by the present Duke of Norfolk.

Newcastle. After the battle of Marston Moor it was retaken, and the castle demolished by order of the Parliament, 1648.

Sheffield has given to the world several names of note, among whom may be mentioned Ebenezer Elliott, who was a Sheffield man, though not, strictly speaking, a native of the town, having been born at Masborough. Sheffield claims as her own another poet, who was not a native. James Montgomery was born at Irvine, in Ayrshire, in 1771, but spent the greater part of his life at Sheffield, where he died in 1854. For about half a century he was editor of the *Sheffield Iris;* and his staunch adherence to liberal principles twice subjected him to fine and imprisonment. He beguiled the tediousness of his confinement by writing a number of poems, which he entitled " Prison Amusements." The people of Sheffield have shewn their respect for both poets by erecting handsome monuments to their memory.

Sheffield was the birthplace of Mrs. Hofland, authoress of " The Son of a Genius," and numerous other works. Her series of books written for the young are deservedly popular. She was born in 1770, and died in 1844.

John Pye Smith, D.D., was born at Sheffield in 1775. He was educated at the Independent College, Rotherham. His refutation of the Socinian heresy, in a work entitled " The Scripture Testimony to the Messiah," gained him the degree of D.D. (from Yale College, America), and a high reputation as a theologian, which he maintained in subsequent works. For fifty years he discharged the duties of Theological Professor at Homerton College. He died in 1851.

Sir Francis Chantrey, the eminent sculptor, was born in this neighbourhood in 1781, and died in 1841.

Mark Firth, who died in 1880, amassed a large fortune as a steel manufacturer here, and he spent a considerable portion of it in works of charitable munificence. Chief amongst his benefactions were the presentation of 36 acres of land, in the north-east of the town, as a public park ; the foundation and partial endowment of Firth College, in the centre of the town, for the benefit of students who wished to continue their course beyond the ordinary school period ; and the erection and endowment of almshouses at Ranmoor at a cost of £30,000.

SHEFFIELD—POPULATION AND MANUFACTURES.

Sheffield is the second town in Yorkshire in point of population and commercial importance, Leeds occupying the first place. Since the beginning of the present century, the population of Sheffield has been more than quintupled. In 1801 it was 45,755; in 1841, 111,091; in 1851, 135,310; and in 1871, 239,946. At the census of 1881 the population of the borough, which covers an area of 19,651 acres, was 284,508—males 141,298, females 143,210—showing an increase during the previous ten years of $18\frac{1}{2}$ per cent. It is represented in Parliament by five members.

Sheffield owes its first establishment and its extraordinary development to its great natural advantages, combined with the energy and enterprise of its citizens. The value of the five rapid and manageable streams which converge towards the town from the surrounding hills must have been immense in the days when steam-power was yet unknown. These streams turn numerous grinding-wheels, which are situated in every favourable position, and, with the rather rough-looking men who work with them, form highly picturesque objects.* But its abundant water-power is one of the smallest, and, in these days, least important advantages of Sheffield. Abundance of coal, of the kinds best suited for the different operations of the Sheffield manufacturers, is to be found in the vicinity. Iron ore is abundant. Building stone, capable of bearing the great heat of the furnaces, and clay for bricks and melting-pots, are also obtained in plenty in the neighbourhood.

In the thirteenth century Sheffield had gained some reputation by its iron manufactures, its "whittles"† finding their way into the southern and eastern counties. In the reign of Queen Elizabeth many artisans emigrated from the Netherlands into England, in consequence of the cruelties of the Duke of Alva, and the iron workers settled in Sheffield, thereby giving a great impetus to the trade. From this period the town began to be noted for the manufacture of shears, sickles, knives, and scissors.

* " Beautiful rivers of the desert ! ye
Bring food for labour from the foodless waste.
Pleased stops the wanderer on his way, to see
The frequent weir oppose your heedless haste,
Where toils the mill, by ancient woods embraced.
Hark, how the cold steel screams in hissing fire !
There draws the grinder his laborious breath ;
There, coughing at his deadly trade, he bends."—*Elliott.*

† " A Sheffield whittle bare he in his hose."—*Chaucer.*

Sheffield, with its neighbourhood, is the chief seat of the steel manufacture. The greater part of the iron here turned into steel is imported from northern Europe. The iron of Sweden, Norway, and Russia, is much superior for steel purposes to that produced in this country; and vast quantities are received annually in the port of Hull, and forwarded to Sheffield, to be there turned into the numberless articles of utility and ornament for the production of which this town is so famous. It is not within our province to give a detailed account of the manufactures of Sheffield. Some establishments confine themselves to the preliminary process of converting the iron into steel; others to the beating of the bars into a higher and finer quality; others to "milling" and "rolling." Some establishments, again, unite all these operations. In the final manufacture of the steel into articles of commerce, some houses produce almost every article, while others direct their attention chiefly to one branch. Many of these establishments are of vast size, but the steel manufacture is not confined to them; for in the surrounding district there are villages of cutlers, fork-makers, and file-cutters, and in many a cottage, with its little patch of land attached, there is a forge for the manufacture of a particular sort of knife. Cutlery, in all its branches, is the chief manufacture of Sheffield. Plated goods are also one of its staple manufactures. Brass foundries are numerous. Buttons, wire, fenders, grates, boilers, spoons, tea and coffee pots, candlesticks, and other articles of Britannia metal, are made in great quantities. The manufacture of steel springs for railway carriages is an important industry. Among the larger steel works are the Brightside, the Bessemer, the River Don, the Scotia, and the Atlas. Messrs. Rodgers and Sons are famed for cutlery. Walker and Hall enjoy a world-wide reputation for silver-plating, which was discovered mainly by the late Mr. Walker. The showrooms at the larger establishments are worth a visit. In some cases an order may be secured to visit the manufactories.

Sheffield is built upon an amphitheatre of hills. The streets are consequently undulating, and occasionally precipitous. The central thoroughfares contain handsome shops; and there are many fine villa residences and suburban mansions.

ST. PETER'S CHURCH, a handsome building, on an open site which displays it to much advantage, is the only object of any antiquity in the town. There was a church here in the time of Henry I.; but the oldest parts of the present edifice do not seem to be of earlier date than the reign of Edward III. It consists of nave, aisles, chancel, and two transepts, with a beautiful crocketed spire. The transepts were added in 1880, when the fabric was thoroughly restored at a cost of £20,000. At the same time the nave was lengthened and two porches placed at the west end. In the south transept three stained glass windows were placed. The galleries were removed, and the high old-fashioned pews in the body of the church replaced by oaken seats. On October 26, 1880, the church was reopened by the Archbishop of York.

The interior contains some interesting monuments, including a bust, the first known work of Sir Francis Chantrey, of the Rev. J. Wilkinson, a former Vicar of Sheffield. This fine work has in it unmistakable indications of the genius and success which crowned the career of that great sculptor. The part of the chancel on the right hand from the altar forms the sepulchral chapel of the Talbot family, commonly called the Shrewsbury Chapel. The most imposing monument here is that of George, the sixth Earl of Shrewsbury. It is massive in form, and Grecian in style. Above a sarcophagus lies a full-length figure of the earl in armour, with his helmet behind his head. Beside the sculptured helmet lies an old one of metal, broken and rusty, probably a relic of the deceased. At his feet is another of the same description. On the stone above is a long Latin inscription in gilt letters, written by John Fox, the martyrologist, setting forth the noble origin, personal dignities, and public and private virtues of the earl.

Near the altar is the monument of George, the fourth earl, and his two countesses. It is finely sculptured. The effigies of the earl and his two wives are beautifully executed in marble. This tomb is under an arch of a peculiar form, which has been very properly preserved on the restoration and alteration of the interior of the church.

It is a fact worth recording, in connection with this church, that William Walker, who is commonly supposed to have been the executioner of Charles I., is interred in the chancel, close to the door, on the south side. There was formerly a brass affixed to the wall, with an inscription to his memory; but this has long

---

* Hunter's "History of Hallamshire,"

disappeared. The inscription, however, has been preserved; and a copy of it will be found in Hunter's book, in which it is shewn conclusively that William Walker was not a likely person to undertake the office of an executioner, although from his translating the "*Vindiciæ contra Tyrannos*," and his friendship with leading members of the republican party, it is very probable that he considered the execution of Charles a thing entirely right. At the Restoration, Walker retired to Darnall, in this parish, where he died in 1700. His burial is entered in the old register of the church.

There are about twenty other churches in Sheffield, but they do not require to be individually referred to, as, though many of them very handsome buildings, they are not, from their antiquity or otherwise, of much general interest.

Among the dissenting places of worship is a new *Roman Catholic Church*, a building of much magnificence. There is a *Wesleyan College*, a spacious and splendid edifice, a little out of the town, on the Manchester road.

Public buildings of a municipal, educational, and miscellaneous character, are numerous, and of a style worthy of this great and prosperous town. The more important of these are—the *Town Hall, Corn Exchange*, the *School of Art*, the *Ruskin Museum*, the *Mappin Picture Gallery*, the *General Post-Office*, the *Public Baths, Infirmary, Shrewsbury Hospital, Jessop Hospital, Banks, Firth, Ranmoor*, and *Wesley Colleges*. In the suburbs there is an attractive *Botanic Garden*.

A monument to Ebenezer Elliott stands in Weston Park. It consists of a bronze statue of the poet, in a sitting posture. A handsome monument has been raised to James Montgomery in the *Cemetery*. The Crimean Column is in Union Street.

Sheffield is remarkably well supplied with recreation grounds. The Duke of Norfolk, besides presenting three plots of ground for recreation, has granted to the town the use of *Norfolk Park*, 60 acres in extent. The *Weston Park* and *Museum*, occupying the grounds and mansion-house of Weston Hall, was purchased in 1873 for £25,000. The grounds are about 13 acres in extent, and the Museum includes—in addition to the Mappin Art Gallery, erected 1887 at a cost of £15,000, and containing the Mappin bequest of pictures valued at £80,000—a natural history collection, and a collection of antiquities. In addition to the *Firth Park*, opened in 1875, 32 acres of land at Endcliffe were acquired in 1887. The *Botanical Gardens* (18 acres), in the western suburbs, belong to a company, but on certain days are open at a small charge. The *Bramall Lane Cricket-Ground* is the scene of many of the Yorkshire county matches.

VICINITY OF SHEFFIELD.

Once out of the smoke and noise of Sheffield, the tourist will find that it is pleasantly situated, and that its busy workers may soon find themselves, when the intermission of their labour admits of it, amid attractive scenery. The manufacturing towns, with which the railway connects Sheffield, are elsewhere described, and need not be here again referred to.

SHERWOOD FOREST.—The reader of Scott will scarcely require to be reminded that many of the scenes of "Ivanhoe" are laid in the tract of country in the neighbourhood of Sheffield and Rotherham. "In that pleasant district of merry England which is watered by the Don," begins Sir Walter, "there extended in ancient times a large forest, covering the greater part of the beautiful hills and valleys which lie between Sheffield and the pleasant town of Doncaster. The remains of this extensive wood are still to be seen at the noble seats of Wentworth, of Wharncliffe Park, and around Rotherham. Here haunted of yore the fabulous Dragon of Wantley; here were fought many of the most desperate battles during the civil wars of the Roses; and here also flourished in ancient times those bands of gallant outlaws whose deeds have been rendered so popular in English song."

Sherwood Forest extended in ancient times from Nottingham to Whitby, 100 miles in a straight line. So late as the time of Queen Elizabeth, it contained a space equal to the present dimensions of the New Forest. There are considerable remains of it near Mansfield in Nottinghamshire, and there is enough of fine and old wood remaining in this part of the West Riding to which Scott refers, to help the tourist to realise the truth of the charming description of sylvan scenery with which "Ivanhoe" opens. The tourist will doubtless be glad to recal the scene in which Wamba, the son of Witless, and Gurth, with his herd of porkers, make their first appearance :—" The sun was setting upon one of the rich grassy glades of that forest which we have mentioned in the beginning of the chapter. Hundreds of broad-headed, short-stemmed, wide-branched oaks, which had witnessed perhaps the stately march of the Roman soldiery, flung their gnarled arms over a thick carpet of the most delicious greensward; in some places they were intermingled with beeches, hollies, and copsewood of various descriptions, so closely as totally to intercept the level beams of the sinking sun; in others they receded from each other, forming those long sweeping vistas, in the intricacy of which the eye delights to lose itself, while imagination considers them as the paths to yet wilder scenes of sylvan solitude. Here the red rays of the sun shot a broken and discoloured light, that partially hung upon the shattered boughs and mossy trunks of the trees, and there they illuminated in brilliant patches the portions of turf to which they made their way."

WENTWORTH HOUSE, the princely seat of the Earl of Fitzwilliam, is four miles from Rotherham. When the family are absent the house and grounds are freely shown to visitors, but inquiries should be made as to this. For extent and magnificence it can be equalled by few private residences in the kingdom. The principal front is to the park, and consists of a centre and two wings. In the centre six Corinthian columns rise from a rusticated stylobate, and support an angular pediment, with the motto and arms of the Marquis of Rockingham (the mansion having been erected by the first marquis, who died in 1750). The pediment is surrounded by three statues, one at each angle. The rest of the building corresponds admirably in style with the centre.

The *Entrance Hall* is very large and lofty, and contains some good sculptures, chiefly copies in marble from the famous antiques. Among them is the Venus de Medicis.

The collection of paintings is valuable. It includes works by Vandyck, Titian, Salvator Rosa, Sir Peter Lely, and numerous other celebrated painters. We give the names of the principal pictures.

First Room. Vandyck—Three children of the unfortunate Earl of Strafford. Sir Joshua Reynolds—Full-length portrait of Charles, Marquis of Rockingham.

Library. Vandyck's famous painting of Lord Strafford and his Secretary. Sir Peter Lely—Lady Anne and Lady Arabella Wentworth.

Gallery. Sir Peter Lely—Two Children. Vandyck—Henrietta Maria; Rinaldo and Armido. Salvator Rosa—Jason and the Dragon; a rocky sea-coast. Teniers—A landscape, with peasants. Vandyck—Lord Strafford in armour. Raphael—Virgin and Child (a copy, Waagen says). Titian—A holy family. Palma Vecchio—Virgin and Child, with the Baptist and St. Catherine. Van Ostade—Peasant Wedding. Claude Lorraine—Landscape. Sir Joshua Reynolds—Portrait of the Countess Fitzwilliam, mother of the present Earl. Sir Godfrey Kneller—Portrait of Shakspeare, a copy, presented by Sir Godfrey to Dryden (having the same features as the Chandos picture in the Bridgewater Gallery).

Yellow Damask Room. Hogarth—Family of the Earl of Rockingham.

Drawing Room. Sir Joshua Reynolds—Present Earl, when four years of age. Sir Thomas Lawrence—Father of the present Earl. Stubbs—A horse, size of life.

Vandyck Room. Vandyck—Earl of Strafford, in armour; William Laud, Archbishop of Canterbury; Henrietta Maria; Arabella, second Countess of Lord Strafford. Sir Peter Lely—Duke of Gloucester, son of Charles I.; Prince Rupert. Sir Joshua Reynolds—The infant Hercules strangling the Serpents. Jacob Jordaens—A Girl and Old Man. Paul Veronese—The Tribute Money. Titian—A Magdalen.

We have not space to mention other pictures; neither can we particularise the other valuable objects of art with which this noble residence is adorned.

The Park has an area of upwards of 1500 acres, and is adorned with wood and water in a style worthy of the mansion.

The *Mausoleum* of Charles, Marquis of Rockingham, is in the park, to the south of the mansion, and near the grand entrance from the Rotherham road. It is ninety feet high, and consists of three storeys. The basement storey is square, and Doric in style; the next is of the same form, but Ionic, each of its four sides opening into an arch; and the third storey consists of twelve Ionic columns supporting a cupola. The arches in the second storey disclose to view a beautiful sarcophagus standing in the centre. Over the arches is the following inscription:—"This monument was erected by Wentworth, Earl Fitzwilliam, 1788, to the memory of Charles, Marquis of Rockingham." The lower storey, which consists of an apartment rising into a dome, contains a white marble statue of the marquis in his robes, by

Nollekens. On the pedestal, besides an enumeration of his titles, and a tribute in verse by Frederick Montague, Esq., there is a eulogium on the public and private character of this great statesman from the pen of Edmund Burke. This inscription is too long to be quoted entire. The following is its first paragraph :—

"A man worthy to be held in remembrance, because he did not live for himself. His abilities, industry, and influence were employed, without interruption, to the last hour of his life, to give stability to the liberties of his country; security to its landed property; increase to its commerce; independence to its public councils, and concord to its empire. These were his ends. For the attainment of these ends, his policy consisted in sincerity, fidelity, directness, and constancy. In opposition, he respected the principles of government; in administration he provided for the liberties of the people. He employed his moments of power in realising everything that he had professed in a popular situation, the distinguishing mark of his public conduct. Reserved in profession, sure in performance, he laid the foundation of a solid confidence."

In niches in the wall, there are busts in white marble of Edmund Burke, the Duke of Portland, Frederick Montague, Sir George Saville, Charles James Fox, Admiral Keppel, John Lee, and Lord George Cavendish.

The Marquis of Rockingham was uncle to Earl Fitzwilliam, who succeeded to the estates on his death.

The *Village* is picturesque. A new church was erected in 1873 by Earl Fitzwilliam and his brother to the memory of their father and mother.

WHARNCLIFFE LODGE is about 7 miles from Sheffield. It is generally open to the public on Mondays, Wednesdays, and Saturdays. The station is Oughty Bridge, on the M. S. and L. line. Small and unpretending in its appearance, it yet occupies one of the most beautiful positions of any edifice in the county. Lady Mary Wortley Montague resided here during the early years of her married life, and here her son was born. Writing afterwards from Avignon, and speaking of the exquisite landscape that lies spread out before the eye from the height crowned by the old Castle of the Popes, she describes it as "the most beautiful land prospect I ever saw, *except Wharncliffe.*"

The lodge and estate are the property of Lord Wharncliffe,

and under the charge of a keeper, who, we believe, affords the necessary accommodation for pic-nic or pleasure parties. There is nothing about the building itself deserving of special notice. Close to the lodge is a large ground-fast stone, " in burthen at least a hundred cart loads," as John Taylor, the water-poet, has observed. The stone is about 12 feet long by 6 wide. It bears an inscription, now illegible, but which was deciphered by Mr. Hunter as follows :—

"Pray for the saule of
Thomas Wryttelay Knyght
for the Kyngys bode to Edward
the furthe Rychard therd Hare the vii. & Hare viii.
hows saules God perdon wyche
Thomas cawsyd a loge to be made
hon this crag ne mydys of
Wanclife for his plesor to her the
hartes bel in the yere of owr
Lord a thousand ccccc.x."

Some accounts say that this Sir Thomas was fonder of hearing the hart's bell than he was of hearing the sounds of human life and industry, and that he cleared away a whole village on the moor between Sheffield and Penistone, " to lengthen out his chase." At the lodge are preserved the boots worn by Sir Francis Wortley at the battles of Marston Moor and Naseby. He was taken prisoner during the civil wars, and died in the Tower of London.

The view from the summit of the Wharncliffe Crags is extensive and magnificent in the highest degree. Westward, the eye ranges over an expanse of wood, with the Don beneath, and pleasant hills beyond, the distance being closed in by wild moorland. To the south stretches a wide and beautiful valley, the rich green of its bottom, through which the stream pleasantly wanders, contrasting with the dark brown of the bold hills that rise on either side. More cultivated and quietly beautiful is the vale of the Loxley, to the east. The whole view is extremely picturesque, presenting features of the most varied kind.

Wharncliffe will possess an additional interest to some visitors, from the fact of its being generally supposed to be the scene of the ballad entitled, " The Dragon of Wantley," published in Bishop Percy's "Reliques of Antient English Poetry." The ballad is a burlesque (Dr. Percy and other critics are of opinion) upon a contest at law between an overgrown Yorkshire attorney and a gentleman of this neighbourhood. The attorney having, among other dishonest and disreputable actions, deprived three orphans of their inheritance, this gentleman generously took up their cause. He completely defeated his antagonist; and—strangest part of the whole—the attorney broke his heart with vexation at his defeat! More Hall, mentioned in the following extract, is on the opposite side of the Don from Wharncliffe. In the Wharncliffe Crags, near the summit, is a cave, which, in accordance with the "foregone conclusion" of the ballad, is called the Dragon's Cave.

" In Yorkshire, near fair Rotherham,
  The place I know it well;
Some two or three miles, or thereabouts,
  I vow I cannot tell:
But there is a hedge, just on the hill edge,
  And Matthew's house hard by it;
O there and then was this dragon's den,
  You could not choose but spy it.

" Old stories tell how Hercules
  A dragon slew at Lerna,
With seven heads and fourteen eyes,
  To see and well discern-a;
But he had a club, this dragon to drub,
  Or he had ne'er done it, I warrant ye;
But More of More Hall, with nothing at all,
  He slew the dragon of Wantley."

GENERAL DESCRIPTION
AND HISTORY OF THE COUNTY OF YORK.

YORKSHIRE is the largest county in England, exceeding by upwards of six hundred square miles the combined areas of Lincolnshire and Devonshire, which rank next to it in extent. In point of population it is inferior only to Lancashire and the metropolitan county of Middlesex. The outline is an irregular quadrangle, marked out by great natural boundaries. Its whole east side is washed by the German Ocean; on the north, the Tees separates it from Durham; on the south, the Humber divides it from Lincoln; while a range of hills on the west almost exactly defines its limits towards Westmorland and Lancashire.

The lands of Yorkshire slope to the east and south, in accordance with their internal structure. With only one or two slight exceptions, such as the "Whinstone Dike" and "Whin Sill," the mineral masses are regularly stratified; they are not, however, horizontal, but inclined to the eastward, receiving their axis of elevation from a great line of dislocation nearly coincident with the western boundary of the county. The surface of the county may be divided into distinctly-marked natural districts, each of which has superficial characteristics of scenery, as well as an internal formation, peculiarly its own. In the centre of the county, stretching from the Tees to the Humber, is the great Vale of York, a beautiful and fertile tract upon the New Red Sandstone series, bordered on the east by the Lias, and on the west by the

Gunnerside in Swaledale

Magnesian Limestone. The bold and picturesque scenery of the western hills and dales is due to the harder rocks of the Millstone Grit series and the Scar Limestone, which here come to the surface. In the south-western part of the county we have a considerable tract of the Coal formation, the site of the great manufacturing towns of the West Riding, and densely peopled throughout. The north-eastern district is of the Oolitic and Lias formations; and the south-eastern district, with its smooth green wolds, is of Chalk. Between these districts lies the Vale of Pickering, which in prehistoric times was either a river course or a lake opening to the sea. The formation of this tract is of Kimmeridge clay, covered by lacustrine and river deposits. In the portion of the south-eastern district, which is called Holderness, the chalk gives place to a perishable formation of sand, gravel, clay, and lake and river sediment, on which the sea makes constant and easy encroachments.

"The main external features of Yorkshire," says Professor Phillips, "are strictly explicable on the simplest possible theory: viz., that of the long continued action of the agitated sea on the strata which composed its bed, at the time when this bed was raised to constitute land. These strata, by their various degrees of consolidation and peculiarities of position, offered unequal resistance to the waves, and have been unequally wasted; the softer strata, which suffered most waste, have left the greatest hollows—the red marls and blue lias having been excavated in the Vale of York, the Kimmeridge clays in the Vale of Pickering, the limestone shales in Craven, and the tertiary sands in Holderness; while harder masses of chalk constitute the wolds, oolites and sandstones form the moorlands of Whitby, still firmer sandstones and limestones, with some slaty and some basaltic masses, constitute the higher regions of the west.

"To geological differences on a large scale we thus clearly trace the main distinctive features of the great natural divisions of Yorkshire. The mineral qualities and positions of rocks, with the accidents to which they have been subjected, give us the clue to the forms of mountains and valleys, the aspect of waterfalls and rocks, the prevalent herbage, and the agricultural appropriation. Even surface colour and pictorial effect are not fully understood without geological inquiry. While limestone 'scars' support a sweet green turf, and slopes of shale give a stunted growth of bluish sedge, gritstone 'edges' are often deeply covered by brown heath, and abandoned to grouse, the sportsman, or the peat-cutter. In a word, geological distinctions are nowhere more boldly marked than in Yorkshire, or more constantly in harmony with the other leading facts of physical geography."

Perhaps no county in England possesses such varied and interesting scenery, whether sea-coast or inland. From the lofty summits of Mickle Fell, Whernside, Ingleborough, and the other hills in the western range, down to the level and extensive Vale of York, and eastward to the chalk wolds over the Humber, the high moors above the Esk, and the indented sea-coast beyond, there is a succession of scenery presenting every order of beauty, from the wildest sublimity to the gentlest loveliness. The dales of Yorkshire are acknowledged to be unequalled by any others in the kingdom ; and some of them, in the more remote parts of the county, present, both in their scenery and their inhabitants, attractions of no ordinary kind to the adventurous tourist.

The climate, like the soil, varies in different places. The western moors and dales have a bracing climate, the cold being more severe than on the eastern heights. The climate of the central part of the county is equable and healthy. The highest points are Mickle Fell, in the north-west angle of the county, 2600 feet above the sea ; Whernside, 2384 ; Ingleborough, 2361 ; and other hills of rather less altitude in the west ; and Burton Head, 1485, in the north-east. The waters of Yorkshire, with the exception of that very small part of the county on the west slope of the Pennine chain which is drained by the Ribble, all find their way to the eastern sea at points within the limits of the county. The principal rivers unite in the Humber. They are—the Don, Calder, Aire, Wharfe, Nid, Ure, Swale, Derwent, and Hull. The Esk has its own outfall to the sea, as has also the Tees, which forms the northern boundary of the county.

The earliest inhabitants of Yorkshire, of whom we have any record, were the Brigantes, one of the most powerful British tribes. Their territories appear to have included Yorkshire and Lancashire, with perhaps portions of the neighbouring counties. Cartismandua, who delivered up the heroic Caractacus to the Romans, A. D. 51, was queen of this tribe. This action probably conciliated the Romans for a time ; for the Brigantes were not reduced under the power of that nation till the reign of

Vespasian, in the year 71. When Constantine divided Britain into three parts, Yorkshire was included in *Maxima Cæsariensis*. Under the Saxons it formed part of the kingdom of Northumberland, having the name of Deira, when that kingdom was divided into two parts. Along with the rest of the kingdom of Northumbria, Yorkshire yielded to Egbert, king of the West Saxons, about the year 827. On the invasion of the Danes, Yorkshire was reduced after some sanguinary conflicts, in one of which the rival Saxon kings, Osbert and Ella, too late in uniting against the common foe, were slain at York, in 867. Seventy years later, Athelstan " of earls the lord, of heroes the bracelet giver," defeated the Danes in a bloody battle, and brought Northumbria again under Saxon rule. Again and again the Danes renewed the contest, as their fleets landed fresh troops of hardy Northmen on the English coast. The last great struggle was fought in 1066. Hadrada, king of Norway, entered the Humber with 500 ships, and landed an army, which, with that of the Danish prince Tosti, who had invited him, amounted to 60,000 men. Marching upon York, the invaders speedily took it by storm. Harold, the Saxon king of England, at once marched towards York to oppose the invaders, who withdrew, and took up a strong position at Stamford Brig. The dauntless Harold at once attacked them. The battle raged from seven in the morning till three in the afternoon, and issued in the death of Hadrada and Tosti, and the almost total destruction of their army. Three weeks later, Harold had to resist another invader ; and the " last of the Saxons " perished on the field of Hastings. William the Conqueror pursued the same policy towards Yorkshire as towards the rest of the kingdom. He garrisoned York, and bestowed the castles and manors throughout the county on his followers. Several risings against the Norman power, which took place in this county, were punished with great severity. The first parliament mentioned in history, was held in York, by Henry II., in 1160. Many of the principal facts in the history of the county after this period fall to be noticed in that of its chief city, which continued for a long period to be the scene of many of the most important events in our national history.

During the wars of the Roses, Yorkshire was the scene of various important struggles, the chief of which were the battles of Wakefield in 1460, and of Towton in 1461. The suppression of monastic houses by Henry VIII. gave rise to a serious rebellion, commonly called the "Pilgrimage of Grace," in 1536. Several smaller risings occurred shortly after this period; but they were easily and summarily suppressed. Yorkshire was the theatre of many struggles between the royalists and parliamentarians. It was at Marston Moor that the important battle was fought which gave a blow to the fortunes of the haughty and unfortunate Charles, from which they never recovered. With the exception of some royal visits, and several risings in the manufacturing districts, occasioned by commercial distress and the introduction of machinery, the subsequent history of this county presents no events deserving special notice.

Yorkshire contains numerous remains of the peoples who have successively ruled it. The Brigantes or Highlanders—that being the meaning of their name—have left traces of themselves in the names of many of the rivers, and some of the mountains and ancient sites of population; in their tumuli, containing bones, weapons, and ornaments, to be seen on the Wolds and elsewhere; in their camps, such as antiquarians trace at Barwick in Elmet, Hutton Ambo, and Langton; in their stone monuments; and in their pottery.

The Romans have left very numerous and distinct memorials of themselves. Their military roads traverse the county in various directions. One great line enters Yorkshire near Bawtry, crosses the Don at Doncaster (*Danum*), the Aire at Castleford (*Legeolium*), and the Wharfe at Tadcaster (*Calcaria*), and reaches York (*Eboracum*), whence it passes in a north-westerly direction to Aldborough (*Isurium*), then to Catterick Bridge (*Cataractonium*), where it crosses the Swale, and passing still north, leaves the county by crossing the Tees at Pierse Bridge. A little to the north of Catterick, a branch of the road goes off to the left to Greta Bridge, whence it proceeds towards Carlisle. From Eboracum, a road in many places well marked goes eastward by *Derventio* (Malton) and *Delgovitia*, to *Praetorium* (Dunsley). From Isurium several lines of road branch off; one, very distinctly marked, proceeding in a south-westerly direction, crossing the Nid, Wharfe, and Aire, and following the course of the Ribble towards Preston. Roman camps are numerous. The earliest of their stations appears to have been at Aldborough. Traces, more or less distinct, may be seen of camps at York, Bainbridge, Catterick Bridge, Greta Bridge, Stainmoor, Malton, and Cawthorne; while the names and positions of numerous other places, taken in conjunction with the geography of Ptolemy and the itineraries of Antoninus, make it evident that they were Roman settlements. Relics of the Romans have been frequently found, in the shape of votive altars, stone coffins, pavements, sculptures, coins, ornaments of glass, coral, bronze, gold and silver, etc.*

The Anglo-Saxons and Danes are not without their monuments. These are chiefly mounds, raised either for defence or as memorials for the fallen brave. Warlike weapons and ornaments of various kinds have been found in these mounds. The remains of Saxon architecture which Yorkshire possesses consist chiefly of a few pillars, arches, and inscriptions, preserved by being incorporated with later structures. These, which are chiefly in churches, are very interesting. Norman remains are more numerous, and are to be found in much purity and perfection in various castles and ecclesiastical edifices. There are many old fortresses in this county, which are interesting alike for the antiquity of their erection and their historical associations. Its stately minsters, still preserved in their old magnificence, its ancient churches, and the grand ruins of its crumbling abbeys, present abundant and excellent materials for a study and comparison of the different orders of architecture.

This extensive county has given to the world many eminent names. The principal natives of Yorkshire who figure prominently in public affairs, in ancient times, are: Richard Plantagenet, third Duke of York, whose ambition and fate are

---

* EARLY INHABITANTS.—The researches in the tumuli of the wolds and moors, conducted through several years by the Rev. Canon Greenwell of Durham, and with him Sir John Lubbock, Bart. (author of *Pre-Historic Times*); John Evans, Esq., F.R.S., F.S.A., of Hemel Hempstead; Mr. Monkman, Malton; and the Rev. Fred. Porter, Yedingham, have shown that in prehistoric times two races of people inhabited Yorkshire. The earlier race (so thought) was peculiar for long heads (dolicho-cephalic), and buried in long barrows mostly, and had the plainest of pottery, and nothing but stone or flint weapons and implements. Another race, of round heads (brachy-cephalic), buried in round barrows, had a knowledge of metal, implements of bronze being found with their interments, along with ornate pottery and flint implements. The Rev. Canon Greenwell has published a work on the prehistoric people, under the title *A Decade of Skulls from Ancient Northumbria*. Recent excavations at Ulrome, near Driffield, have brought to light an extensive prehistoric lake-dwelling, with some implements of a previously unknown type.

celebrated by Shakspere in "King Henry VI.;" Richard Scroop, also immortalized by Shakspere, beheaded for high treason in 1405; John Fisher, Bishop of Rochester, and afterwards Cardinal, born in 1458, and beheaded, for his opposition to Henry VIII., in 1535; Sir William Gascoigne, the chief justice who committed Prince Henry to prison for contempt of court, born 1350, died 1413; Sir William de la Pole, founder of the powerful family of Suffolk—the character of the fourth Earl and first Duke of which family is delineated in "King Henry VI., Part II."—died 1356; Andrew Marvell, the friend of Milton, and the consistent and unswerving advocate of constitutional principles, born 1620, died 1678. In later times, Hull, the place which Andrew Marvell represented in Parliament, has given birth to William Wilberforce, the friend of the slave, and returned him as its representative. He was born in 1759, and died in 1833. Of noted commanders Yorkshire claims—Thomas, Lord Fairfax, the famous parliamentary general, born 1611, died 1671; Sir John Lawson, the celebrated admiral, died in action, after a brilliant career, 1665; Sir Martin Frobisher, knighted for his gallantry in an action with the Spaniards, and killed in an attack on Brest, 1594. Several noted travellers were born in this county: Armigel Waad, styled by Fuller, "the English Columbus," the first Englishman who set foot on the shores of America, died in 1568; Sir Thomas Herbert, who explored many parts of Asia and Africa, and published an account of his travels, was born in 1606, and died in 1682; and Captain James Cook, the circumnavigator of the globe, born 1728, killed by the savages at the Sandwich Islands, 1779.

In literature, Yorkshire presents a vast array of names. Alcuin, the most distinguished scholar of his age, and the friend of Charlemagne, was born about 735, and died 804. Other natives celebrated for their learning are—Roger Ascham, the tutor of Queen Elizabeth, died 1568; Sir Henry Saville, an accomplished Greek scholar, and the founder of two professorships at Oxford, born 1549, died 1622; Dr. Joseph Hill, editor of Schrevelius' Lexicon, born 1625, died 1707; Richard Bentley, the celebrated classical critic, born 1661, died 1742; John Potter, Archbishop of Canterbury, author of the "Antiquities of Greece," born 1674, died 1747; Dr. Conyers Middleton, author of the "Life of Cicero," "Letter from Rome," etc., born 1683, died 1750. Several natives of this county have taken a high place as topographical historians and antiquarians by their works upon different districts of it. The chief names are those of Roger Dodsworth (1585-1654), Ralph Thoresby (1658-1725), Thomas Gent (1691-1778), Dr. Burton (1697-1771), Francis Drake (died 1770), Dr. Young, Rev. J. Hunter, Rev. J. Graves, Rev. J. Tickell, T. Hinderwell, Rev. W. Eastmead, Rev. C. Wellbeloved, G. Poulson, Professor Phillips, John Browne, J. Walbran, etc.* In an enumeration of writers on divinity belonging to this county, an honoured place must be given to John de Wycliffe, "the Morning Star of the Reformation," and the translator of the Bible, born about 1324, died 1384 ; and to Miles Coverdale, the English reformer, born 1499, died 1580. More recent are—Matthew Pool, author of the "Synopsis Criticorum," a classic in biblical interpretation, born 1624, died 1679 ; John Tillotson, Archbishop of Canterbury, whose "Sermons" hold a high place among the literature of the pulpit, born 1630, died 1694 ; Joseph Bingham, author of the "Origines Ecclesiasticae," born 1668, died 1723 ; Beilby Porteous, Bishop of London, author of a "Life of Archbishop Slaker," and various works in theology, and of some elegant poems, born 1731, died 1808 ; Joseph Milner, author of a valuable "History of the Church of Christ," born 1744, died 1820 ; John Pye Smith, D.D., author of "The Scripture Testimony to the Messiah," and other works, born 1775, died 1850. Next let us notice the men of science :—John Smeaton, civil engineer, the architect of Eddystone Lighthouse, was born in 1724, and died in 1792 ; Joseph Priestley, author of numerous works on experimental philosophy and other subjects, born 1733, died 1804 ; John Ellerton Stocks, M.D., a noted botanist, born 1820, died 1854 ; Professor Sedgwick, of Cambridge University, author of "A Synopsis of the Classification of the Palæozoic Rocks," was born about the year 1786. Yorkshire has produced a fair number of poets, though none of them stand in the highest rank. We take the principal names, in the order of time : John Gower, called by Bale "poet laureate," and said to have been the instructor of Chaucer, was the author of various works, written, some in English, others in French and Latin, died in 1402 ; George Sandys, translator of Ovid's Metamorphoses—a work to which Pope declares that English poetry owes much,

* Dr. Thomas Whitaker, the Dugdale of Yorkshire, was not a native of the county, being born in Norfolk in 1759. One or two of the latest of the names enumerated above may also belong to other counties.

was born in 1577, and died in 1643; Edward Fairfax, the translator of Tasso, died in 1632; Sir Robert Stapleton, the translator of Juvenal and other classic poets, and author of some dramatic pieces, died in 1669; William Congreve, the dramatist, was born in 1669, and died in 1729; Sir Samuel Garth, author of "The Dispensary," and other poems, was born in 1671, and died in 1718; William Mason, best known by his dramatic poem of "Caractacus," and his biography of the poet Gray, was born in 1725, and died in 1797; Ebenezer Elliott, the "Corn-Law Rhymer," born 1781, died 1849; Herbert Knowles, best known by his exquisite "Lines written in the Churchyard of Richmond," died at the early age of nineteen, born 1797, died 1816; Monckton Milnes, M.P., author of "Memorials of a Tour in Greece," and three volumes of poems, born 1809. In other departments of literature are—David Hartley, author of "Observations on Man," born 1705, died 1757; John Foster, author of "Essays in a series of Letters," an "Essay on the Evils of Popular Ignorance," etc., born 1770, died 1839; the late Earl of Carlisle, author of a "Diary in Turkish and Greek Waters," born 1802; Edward Baines, M.P., author of a "History of the Cotton Manufacture," born 1806. Several names of novelists occur, all of them females: Mrs. Hofland, author of "The Son of a Genius," and numerous works for the young, born 1770, died 1844; the Brontës—Charlotte, author of "Jane Eyre," "Shirley," and "Vilette," born 1816, died 1855—Emily, author of "Wuthering Heights," born 1819, died 1848—and Agnes, author of "Agnes Grey," and "The Tenant of Wildfell Hall," born 1822, died 1849; Mrs. Gaskell, the biographer of Miss Brontë, and author of "Ruth," "North and South," and other works; Miss Pardoe, author of "The City of the Sultan," "The Romance of the Harem," and numerous other works. To Yorkshire belong the painters—Benjamin Wilson, who flourished about 1760; William Kent, born 1685, died 1748; John Jackson, born 1778, died 1831; William Etty, R.A., born 1787, died 1849; and W. P. Frith, born 1819; the sculptor, John Flaxman, born 1755, died 1826; the engraver, William Lodge, born 1649, died 1689; and the actor, Richard John Smith, of the Adelphi, born 1786, died 1855.

The area of Yorkshire is 6067 square miles, or 3,882,851 statute acres. The population, according to the census of 1861, amounted to 2,033,610, and at the subsequent censuses as follows:—

POPULATION OF YORKSHIRE.

Division.	Area in acres.	Pop. in 1871.	Pop. in 1881.	Persons to acre. 1871.	Persons to acre. 1881.
North Riding	1,361,664	293,278	346,260	0·22	0·25
East Riding	750,828	268,466	315,460	0·36	0·42
West Riding	1,768,380	1,830,815	2,175,314	1·03	1·23
City of York	1,979	43,796	49,530	22·13	25·03
Total of County	3,882,851	2,436,355	2,886,564	0·63	0·74

In 1881 the total number of males was 1,420,001, and of females 1,466,563—the males exceeding the females in the North Riding by 3534.

The county is divided into four parts—viz. the three *Ridings* and the *Ainsty* of York. For parliamentary purposes the West Riding is subdivided into three districts—East returning 6 members, North 5, and South 8. The North Riding returns 4 members, and the East Riding 3. Bradford returns 3 members, Dewsbury 1, Halifax 2, Huddersfield 1, Hull 3, Leeds 5, Middlesbrough 1, Pontefract 1, Scarborough 1, Sheffield 5, Wakefield 1, and York 2. The North Riding contains an area of 2128 square miles, or 1,361,664 acres, and 346,260 persons. The occupations are chiefly agricultural, but mines employ upwards of 8000 persons. The total number of members returned from this Riding is 8. The East Riding, taking along with it the city of York, has an area of 1176 square miles, or 752,807 acres, and a population of 364,990. In this part of the county the number of persons employed in agriculture is almost equal to that of those engaged in every kind of manufacture. Cotton and flax, engines and ships, are the chief manufactures. The total number of members returned by this division of the county is 5. The West Riding is the most important part of the county in point of manufactures and commerce. Its extent is 2763 square miles, or 1,768,380 acres; and its population, 2,175,314. This is the great seat of the woollen and iron manufactures, of which details are given under the principal towns where the manufactures are carried on.

Agriculture is in a medium state of improvement, but is regarded as not so advanced as in Northumberland and Lincolnshire. Yorkshire, however, is more a grazing than an agricultural

AGRICULTURE AND MANUFACTURES.

county. Craven, and the upper parts of the West Riding generally, are purely pastoral, there being scarcely any arable land in cultivation in this Riding, except in the lower districts. In the East Riding and the lower parts of the North Riding there are considerable tracts of good arable ground. Farms are generally small, and let at high rents from year to year. The total number of farmers in Yorkshire, according to the census of 1881, was 27,647 ; of whom 25,232 were males, and 2215 females. Farm labourers were reckoned at 61,861; 58,738 being males, and 3123 females. All these figures show a marked decline in the last twenty years. Cattle are mostly of the short-horned breed ; but there are large numbers of long-horns, and many varieties produced by crosses of these two breeds. Sheep are numerous, and also of different breeds. Yorkshire has long been celebrated for its horses. Many of the most noted racers which have appeared on the turf were bred and trained in this county. The Cleveland bays are highly esteemed as carriage horses. Horses for agricultural and general purposes are bred in great numbers in this county ; and the horse fairs which are held here at stated times are frequented by dealers from all parts of the kingdom, as well as by foreigners.

The mineral productions of Yorkshire are—coal in abundance, iron, lead, copper, alum, slate, limestone (some of it equal, if not superior, to the Derbyshire marble), building stone, etc. There are very valuable mineral waters in various parts of the county. Those of Harrogate and Scarborough have been long celebrated, and are much resorted to.

The East Riding, though containing the important port of Hull, is chiefly dependent on agriculture, and on the attractions of the beautiful watering-places extending along the coast. Until 1850 the North Riding was even less famed for its manufacturing industry, but the discovery of the rich iron ores in the Cleveland and Hambleton districts wrought a complete transformation in its prospects. While mining villages have sprung up in all directions, the town and port of Middlesbrough has been created ; other towns have increased with almost unexampled rapidity ; and Redcar and Saltburn have developed into fashionable seaside resorts. The great centre of Yorkshire industry is, however, in the West Riding, the foundation of its prosperity being the coal and iron field stretching from Leeds on the north to Sheffield in the south. But while iron and steel are the staple industries of Sheffield, and are extensively manufactured in other towns, it is for its woollen and worsted manufactures that the West Riding is chiefly celebrated. The West Riding has almost a monopoly of the worsted manufactures of the United Kingdom. The manufacturing district may be said, roughly, to include the whole of Yorkshire south of the Aire from Leeds to Skipton. It is deeply indented by valleys which originally supplied abundance of water for the mills, but now this is largely supplemented by steam-worked machinery, for which the proximity of immense coal supplies is a great advantage.

About the Author, Andrew Gill: I live in Lancashire, England and have collected early photographs and optical antiques for over forty years. I am a professional 'magic lantern' showman presenting lantern shows and giving talks on Victorian optical entertainments for museums, festivals, special interest groups and universities. I am the owner of the Keasbury-Gordon Photograph Archive.

The photograph captions in this booklet are those printed or hand-written on the original slides or photographs. If you think they are inaccurate or if you have relevant information that I can include in future editions, please contact me.

To purchase prints of selected historical photographs from my archive, visit www.the-keasburygordon-photograph-archive.artistwebsites.com

For a licence to use my historical photographs for commercial purposes, please contact me.

For information about magic lanterns and slides, visit the website of the Magic Lantern Society: www.magiclantern.org.uk

To contact me, email lanternist@ntlworld.com

I have published historical booklets and photo albums on the subjects below. They are available on the internet as printed and ebooks.

Historical travel guides
Jersey in 1921
Norwich in 1880
Doon the Watter
Liverpool in 1886
Nottingham in 1899
Bournemouth in 1914
Great Yarmouth in 1880
Victorian Walks in Surrey

A Victorian Visit to Brighton
A Victorian Visit to Hastings
Newcastle upon Tyne in 1903
Victorian and Edwardian York
Victorian and Edwardian Leeds
The Way We Were: Manchester
Victorian and Edwardian Bradford
Victorian and Edwardian Sheffield
A Victorian Visit to Peel, Isle of Man
Lechlade to Oxford by Canoe in 1875
Guernsey, Sark and Alderney in 1921
A Victorian Tour of South East Devon
The River Thames from Source to Sea
North Devon through the Magic Lantern
A Victorian Visit to Ramsey, Isle of Man
A Victorian Visit to Douglas, Isle of Man
Victorian Totnes through the Magic Lantern
Victorian Whitby through the Magic Lantern
Victorian Walks on the Isle of Wight (Part 1)
Victorian Walks on the Isle of Wight (Part 2)
Victorian London through the Magic Lantern
St. Ives through the Victorian Magic Lantern
Victorian Torquay through the Magic Lantern
Victorian Glasgow through the Magic Lantern
The Way We Were: Wakefield and Dewsbury
The Way We Were: Hebden Bridge to Halifax
Victorian Edinburgh through the Magic Lantern
Victorian Scarborough through the Magic Lantern
The Way We Were: Hull and the surrounding area
The Way We Were: Harrogate and Knaresborough
A Victorian Tour of North Wales: Rhyl to Llandudno
A Victorian Visit to Lewes and the surrounding area
The Isle of Man through the Victorian Magic Lantern
A Victorian Railway Journey from Plymouth to Padstow
A Victorian Visit to Malton, Pickering and Castle Howard
A Victorian Visit to Eastbourne and the surrounding area
A Victorian Visit to Castletown, Port St. Mary and Port Erin
Penzance and Newlyn through the Victorian Magic Lantern
Victorian Brixham and Dartmouth through the Magic Lantern
Victorian Plymouth and Devonport through the Magic Lantern
A Victorian Tour of North Wales: Conwy to Caernarfon via Anglesey
Staithes, Runswick and Robin Hood's Bay through the Magic Lantern
Dawlish, Teignmouth and Newton Abbot through the Victorian Magic Lantern
A Victorian Visit to Cornwall: Morwenstow to Tintagel via Kilkhampton, Bude, Boscastle and Bossiney

Other historical topics
Sarah Jane's Victorian Tour of Scotland
Victorian Street Life through the Magic Lantern
The First World War through the Magic Lantern

Ballyclare May Fair through the Victorian Magic Lantern
The Story of Burnley's Trams through the Magic Lantern
The Franco-British 'White City' London Exhibition of 1908
How they built the Forth Railway Bridge: A Victorian Magic Lantern Show

Historical photo albums
Hull: The Way We Were
The Way We Were: Suffolk
Norwich: The Way We Were
Sheffield: The Way We Were
The Way We Were: Somerset
Doncaster: The Way We Were
Fife through the Magic Lantern
Rotherham: The Way We Were
York through the Magic Lantern
Rossendale: The Way We Were
The Way We Were: Lincolnshire
The Way We Were: Cumberland
Building the Forth Railway Bridge
Burnley through the Magic Lantern
Oban to the Hebrides and St. Kilda
Glasgow through the Magic Lantern
Liverpool through the Magic Lantern
Blackpool through the Magic Lantern
Tasmania through the Magic Lantern
New York through the Magic Lantern
Swaledale through the Magic Lantern
Edinburgh through the Magic Lantern
Llandudno through the Magic Lantern
Manchester through the Magic Lantern
Birmingham through the Magic Lantern
Scarborough through the Magic Lantern
Penzance, Newlyn and the Isles of Scilly
Great Yarmouth through the Magic Lantern
Ancient Baalbec through the Magic Lantern
The Isle of Skye through the Magic Lantern
Ancient Palmyra through the Magic Lantern
The Kentish Coast from Whitstable to Hythe
New South Wales through the Magic Lantern
The River Thames through the Magic Lantern
The River Tyne from Newcastle to Tynemouth
From Glasgow to Rothesay by paddle steamer
Victorian Childhood through the Magic Lantern
The Way We Were: Yorkshire Railway Stations
Southampton, Portsmouth and the Great Liners
Newcastle upon Tyne through the Magic Lantern
Egypt's Ancient Monuments through the Magic Lantern
The Way We Were: Holmfirth, Honley and Huddersfield
The Way We Were: Birkenhead, Port Sunlight and the Wirral
Ancient Egypt, Baalbec and Palmyra through the Magic Lantern

Printed in Great Britain
by Amazon